Michelle Van Tassell

W9-AUE-202

Quiet-Time Busy Books

Fun Fabric Pages
Personalized
for Your Little One

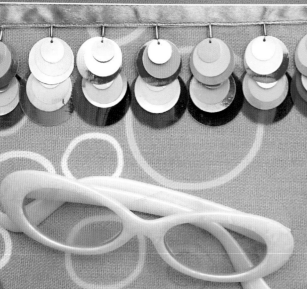

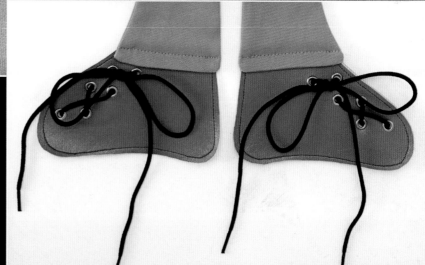

C&T PUBLISHING

Text copyright © 2007 by Michelle Van Tassell

Artwork copyright © 2007 by C&T Publishing, Inc.

Publisher: **Amy Marson**

Editorial Director: **Gailen Runge**

Editor: **Stacy Chamness**

Technical Editors: **Carolyn Aune, Susan Nelsen**

Copyeditor/Proofreader: **Wordfirm Inc.**

Front Cover Designer: **Christina Jarumay**

Design Director/Book Designer: **Rose Sheifer-Wright**

Back Cover Designer: **Kiera Lofgreen**

Production Coordinator: **Tim Manibusan**

Illustrator: **Kirstie L. Pettersen**

Photography by C&T Publishing, Inc., unless otherwise noted

Published by C&T Publishing, Inc., P.O. Box 1456, Lafayette, CA 94549

All rights reserved. No part of this work covered by the copyright hereon may be used in any form or reproduced by any means—graphic, electronic, or mechanical, including photocopying, recording, taping, or information storage and retrieval systems—without written permission from the publisher. The copyrights on individual artworks are retained by the artists as noted in *Quiet-Time Busy Books*. These designs may be used to make items only for personal use or donation to nonprofit groups for sale. Each piece of finished merchandise for sale must carry a conspicuous label with the following information: Designs copyright © 2007 by Michelle Van Tassell from the book *Quiet-Time Busy Books* from C&T Publishing, Inc.

Attention Copy Shops: Please note the following exception—publisher and author give permission to photocopy pages 11, 31, 44-45, 49, and 52 for personal use only.

Attention Teachers: C&T Publishing, Inc., encourages you to use this book as a text for teaching. Contact us at 800-284-1114 or www.ctpub.com for more information about the C&T Teachers' Program.

We take great care to ensure that the information included in our products is accurate and presented in good faith, but no warranty is provided nor are results guaranteed. Having no control over the choices of materials or procedures used, neither the author nor C&T Publishing, Inc., shall have any liability to any person or entity with respect to any loss or damage caused directly or indirectly by the information contained in this book. For your convenience, we post an up-to-date listing of corrections on our website (www.ctpub.com). If a correction is not already noted, please contact our customer service department at ctinfo@ctpub.com or at P.O. Box 1456, Lafayette, CA 94549.

Trademark (™) and registered trademark (®) names are used throughout this book. Rather than use the symbols with every occurrence of a trademark or registered trademark name, we are using the names only in the editorial fashion and to the benefit of the owner, with no intention of infringement.

Library of Congress Cataloging-in-Publication Data

Tassell, Michelle van.
  Quiet-time busy books : fun fabric pages personalized for your little one / Michelle Van Tassell.
    p. cm.
  ISBN-13: 978-1-57120-401-1 (paper trade : alk. paper)
  ISBN-10: 1-57120-401-6 (paper trade : alk. paper)
  1. Self-publishing. 2. Bookbinding. 3. Early childhood education--Parent participation. I. Title.
  Z285.5.T37 2008
  070.5'93--dc22

Printed in China
10 9 8 7 6 5 4 3 2 1

Dedication

To my mother, who can take anything and

make a beautiful something.

To my children, Alexander, Benjamin, Sophia, and Asher,

who inspired and play-tested the ideas in this book.

And to my dear husband, who gave me my children and

who made our home a place of love and fun.

CONTENTS

Getting Started

A Page Can Be Finished in a Day

The pages of this busy book are not bound together, so you have to finish only one page at a time—and a page can be completed in a day. Relatives and friends can contribute to the book, making a tradition of giving new quiet book pages as they are completed. And as children grow, their interests change, and new pages can reflect their development.

When I looked for a cloth busy book for my first child, I couldn't find a pattern that seemed interesting enough to go through the trouble of making. Eventually, I started to design my own books. I now have four children, and in the thirteen years since my first child was born, I've tested my designs on both my own kids and my friends' kids.

Crooked Has Character

My personality is more creative than precise. I love to make things that allow for some quirks (personalization, shall we say?). The busy book pages in this book are easy to make, and in this case, crooked has character. Children aren't critiquing seam lines, and nobody's pants will split if something is a little off. Prefab books available at chain stores around the country are perfect—and boring. Handmade and a little bit crooked make for personality and charm.

A Busy Book Is a True Scrapbook

Stocked with pictures, fabrics, and trinkets from life, a busy book is literally a scrapbook. With digital cameras, scanners, or even the services of a local copy shop, putting pictures on fabric is easy. Children love to see themselves, loved ones, and their favorite things on the pages.

Many Children Can Use the Book Simultaneously

The unbound busy book also makes it possible for many children to use it at the same time. My older kids will begin to help a little one play but regularly end up snatching pages away for their own entertainment. We often see the pages of our book strewn down a row of children.

Definitions

I'll be using these terms throughout the book, so refer to these definitions as necessary.

Background fabric: The base fabric of the page
Bottom-weight cotton: Heavyweight fabric, such as chino, crepe, denim, drapery fabric, gabardine, sailcloth, suiting, tweed, twill, upholstery fabric, wool sateen, worsted wool, and the like

Bottom-weight cotton is best for background fabric.

Edgestitching: A row of stitching close to a seam line, fold line, or finished edge of fabric

Double stitching: A second row of stitching, usually ¼" away from and parallel to the row of edgestitching

Page: An entire quiet book page (front and back layers)
Page face: The front section of the page, where the activity is located

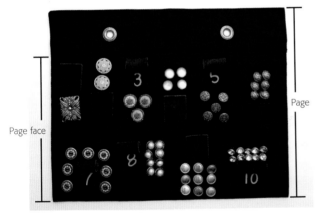

Page face

Page

The page face measures 8½" × 14".

Topstitching: A row of stitching, in matching or contrasting thread, close to a seam line, fold line or finished edge of fabric. Often used as a decorative effect, but can also be functional, as when attaching a pocket.

Supplies

Fabrics

For the background fabric, **bottom-weight cottons** like denim and twill are easiest to work with. Textured fabrics like corduroy can work, but they might shift a little as you sew. Lightweight fabrics like quilter's cottons also work, but the pages will be softer and less durable. Consider using stiff interfacing if you use thin cotton.

TIP

Backgrounds should usually be solid or near solid in appearance. Designs in the background fabric can distract from the activities.

Interfacing

You can use **fast2fuse**, a double-sided fusible stiff interfacing from C&T Publishing (Sources, page 63), or other fusible interfacing. For many of the pages, fusible interfacing is enough to give the page a little weight and to secure the buttonholes, but for some pages, **fast2fuse** is best because it provides added stiffness to the page and makes a great working surface— a perfect little lap table.

Photo Transfers

There are several options for transferring photos to fabric. I prefer to print directly to fabric. Both printing to fabric and using iron-on transfer sheets produce good picture quality, so use the option you prefer. Some differences between the two methods are shown on page 6.

I prefer the cotton poplin Crafter's Images PhotoFabric sheets by Blumenthal Craft (Sources, page 63). They are backed with peel-off paper, so they feed easily through your printer.

	PRINT TO IRON-ON TRANSFER SHEET	PRINT TO FABRIC
PROCESS	Print image to transfer sheet, trim, and iron image to fabric.	Print image directly onto fabric, iron, rinse in water, and iron again.
BACKGROUND OPTIONS	Transfer image to a colored fabric background.	Print on a white or off-white background.
BORDER	Depending on how close you trim, this method leaves a white border around the image.	Print any border you can create on the computer or print with no border at all.
VULNERABILITY	Often sensitive to heat, so ironing without protecting the image can ruin it.	Image can be ironed without a protective sheet.
TEXTURE	Often the iron-on has a plastic-y feel.	The image feels like the fabric it is printed on.
ADHESIVENESS	If you don't round the corners or zigzag the edges, the iron-on can peel off the fabric.	The ink prints directly to the fabric without adding a separate layer.

Sophia Nicole

Age 2

Loves pink, jewelry, and shoes.
Hates seatbelts, tight socks, and sprinklers.
Talks to all passing dogs, and occasionally licks back.
Sucks on two fingers most of the time.
Wants pancakes every morning before the sun comes up.
Wears at least three different outfits every day.
Calls lip gloss "lip sauce" and horses "brown zebras."
Thinks she's as big as her brothers.
Dances to any music.
Runs, hops, splashes.

TIP As long as you're printing out pictures for the page faces, think about printing out labels for the back. Consider including your name, the child's name, the date, and a special message.

To my favorite grandkids.
Love, Grandma
Christmas 2007

Asher's Quiet Book

june '06

for sophia

love, mom

Kids love having personalized labels for the pages.

General Instructions

Pick the page you want to create, and follow the instructions. After you complete the activity, follow the Completing the Page instructions (page 61).

Interfacing Options

For most pages, you can use fast2fuse (Sources, page 63) or other fusible interfacing behind the activity. The edges of the interfacing will be fold lines for the pages. Heavyweight fast2fuse gives your page a real stiffness—it is thick, and though it bends, it holds its shape well and makes a good lap table surface. Regular-weight fast2fuse and other fusible interfacings are less stiff. Always use a lightweight fusible interfacing for the thin strip where the buttonholes will be sewn.

fast2fuse

1. Cut a 15" x 23½" rectangle of the background fabric, or cut it to the size specified for your page.
2. Cut a 2½" × 15" strip of fusible interfacing and a 9" × 14" rectangle of fast2fuse.
3. Iron the strip of interfacing to the wrong side of the fabric. Align the sides of the fabric and the interfacing and place the strip ½" below Edge B.
4. Align the fast2fuse rectangle with Edge A, leaving a ½" margin on each side of the rectangle.

fast2fuse has fusible material on both sides, so use a transfer protection sheet or parchment paper to protect the side you are not fusing.

The fast2fuse rectangle is 1" narrower than the page because you don't need to sew the fast2fuse into the side seams of the page.

Fusible Interfacing

1. Cut a 15" x 23½" rectangle of the background fabric, or cut it to the size specified for your page.
2. Cut a 2½" × 15" strip and a 9" × 15" rectangle of interfacing.
3. Iron the fusible interfacing to the wrong side of the fabric as shown below.

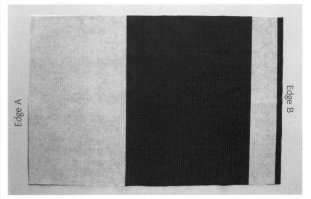

The rectangle is aligned with Edge A and the side edges of the fabric; the strip is aligned with the sides of the fabric, leaving ½" of fabric exposed toward Edge B.

Pocket Instructions

Follow the page-specific instructions for pocket fabric measurements and cutting.

1. To form the top finished pocket edge, press under ¼" along the top edge of the pocket rectangle, wrong sides together.

2. Fold the same edge 1" in the opposite direction, with right sides together. Pin the sides of the folded edge in place.

3. Using ½″ seam allowances, stitch the sides of the folded edge in place. Lengthen the stitch to a basting stitch and continue sewing around the sides and the bottom of the rectangle. Only the top 1″ of the side seams needs to be securely stitched.

4. Clip the top corners.

5. Turn the top edge right side out. Press. Using the basting as a guide, press ½″ under on the sides and bottom of the rectangle. Remove the basting.

Edgestitch the top edge closed; double stitch if you like.

6. Edgestitch ¾″ below the top folded edge, securing the doubled-over edge of the pocket.

7. Follow the page-specific instructions to position the pocket and then topstitch the side and bottom edges to attach the pocket to the page. You can also double stitch ¼″ inside the first line of stitching.

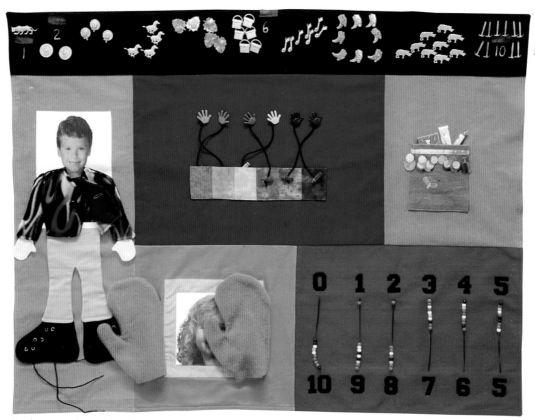

Combine several pages for a floor quilt.

TIP Get a friend to work with and share supplies. Buying fabric for a page often leaves enough for a second one. Working with a friend splits the costs.

Thrift stores are good sources for materials. Cut up old purses, belts, or shoes for leather and buckles. Buy used clothes for interesting buttons you can pull off. Look for interesting or wacky printed fabrics on the racks.

Peek-a-Boo Flaps

This page is simple, but it's always a favorite. Younger kids like to touch the interesting buttons and play with the little flaps. Older kids like to confirm that the number behind the flap is really the same as the number of buttons clustered around it.

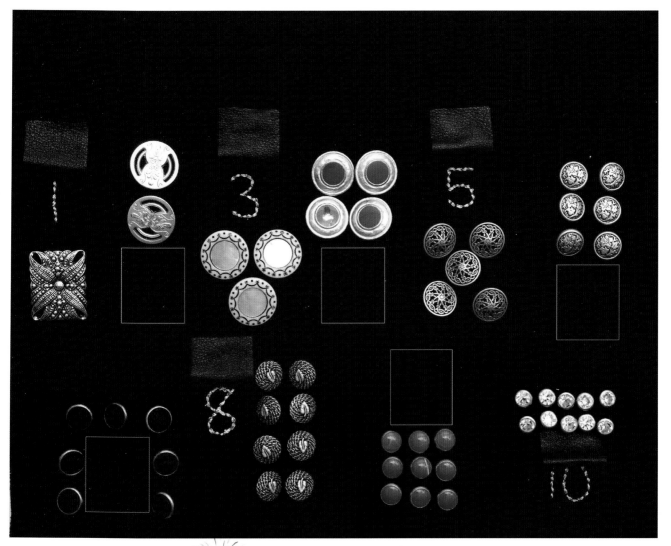

What You'll Need

- ½ yard of bottom-weight background fabric
- ¼ yard of regular fusible interfacing
- Leather for 10 rectangles 1½" × 1¼"
- 55 buttons, ranging from large to small

- Paint pen or embroidery floss
- Thread
- Heavyweight thread to sew on buttons
- Chalk fabric marker

How-To

Cutting

- Cut a 15″ × 23½″ rectangle of cotton fabric.
- Cut interfacing per the instructions on pages 7–8.
- Cut 10 rectangles 1½″ × 1¼″ from the leather.

Assembly

1. **Iron on interfacing.** Follow the instructions for fusible interfacing on page 7.
2. **Arrange buttons and flaps.** Referring to the photo on page 9 and the diagram below, arrange the buttons and leather flaps on the page face, spacing them to fit your particular buttons. Make sure you are working with Edge A at the top. Leave at least a 1″ margin around the top and side edges of the page face and ½″ at the bottom along the edge that will be folded.

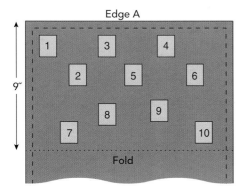

3. **Mark flap positions.** Use a chalk marker to mark around each flap and then remove all the flaps and buttons from the page face.

TIP Buying bags of mixed buttons is often cheaper than buying individual buttons. The buttons in each cluster don't need to be identical. Group buttons that are similar in size and color and don't worry if they are slightly different.

4. **Paint or embroider numbers.** Using a number style of your choice, paint or embroider the numbers, centering each number within the chalked outline of a flap. Center the numbers side-to-side and position them near the bottom of the chalked outline, so there's room to stitch across the top of the flap. Brush to remove the chalk.

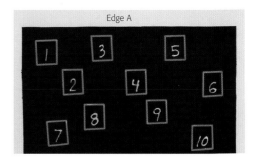

TIP Paint or embroider the numbers in a color that contrasts with the fabric.

5. **Attach leather flaps.** Stitch across the short edge of each flap so that it covers the number, without stitching over or crowding the top.

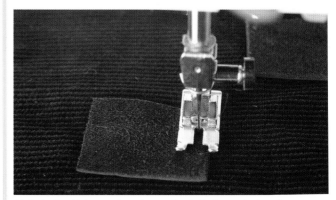

Stitch the flap high enough so the number isn't obscured when the flap is lifted.

6. **Sew on buttons.** Sew the buttons in groups around the flaps as shown in the photo on page 9. Don't worry about following the photo exactly. Make adjustments so that your buttons cluster well.

TIP Remember that these buttons are guaranteed to be pulled and likely to be chewed. Sew them on with heavy thread and a couple extra laps through the shanks.

7. **Finish page.** Follow the Completing the Page instructions (page 61) to finish the page.

TIP Use a solid background fabric that won't compete with the buttons. Keeping the leather and the fabric the same color will also reduce visual clutter. Look for scraps of leather in craft stores or cut into old leather from thrift stores. The black leather in the samples here came from some old biker pants I found. Instead of leather, you can use vinyl or any nonfraying and fairly stiff material.

Use photos and names instead of buttons and numbers.

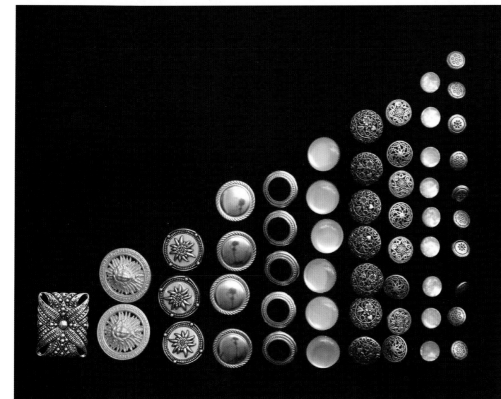

Some of the buttons pictured in the samples came from my grandma's collection. As a new bride in 1938, she was given a Mason jar with a handful of buttons that her mother, aunts, and friends had pulled from worn-out clothes. The edges of these buttons, rubbed thin by many fingers, tell the stories of a life.

The buttons in the jar rotated from old clothes to new and back to old. One of my uncles regularly popped the buttons off his shirts, and Grandma would replace the lost buttons with buttons from the jar. I don't know why she never taught that kid to sew!

Bead Abacus

This primitive abacus teaches counting as well as addition. Eventually, kids understand that when the top has the correct number of beads, the bottom has the correct number too.

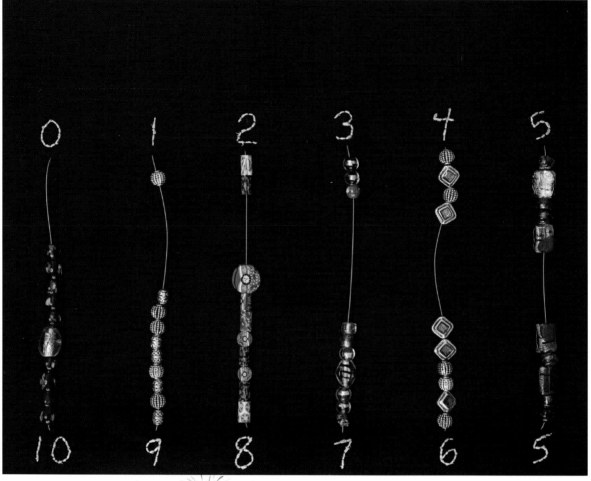

What You'll Need

- ¹/₂ yard of bottom-weight background fabric

- ¹/₄ yard of fast2fuse or regular fusible interfacing (*If using fast2fuse, you also need a 2¹/₂″ × 15″ strip of regular fusible interfacing.*)

- 2 yards of ribbon thin enough to thread through beads

- 60 interesting medium beads in 6 groups of 10

- Paint pen or embroidery floss

- Thread

- Big needle, nail, or awl to poke holes in fabric

- 12 flat buttons (¹/₂″ to ³/₄″ diameter) to secure the ribbon

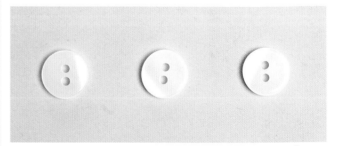

These buttons will be hidden inside to keep the bead strings from pulling through the fabric.

How-To

Cutting

- Cut a 15″ × 23½″ rectangle of cotton fabric.
- Cut the fast2fuse or interfacing per the instructions on pages 7–8.
- Cut 6 lengths of ribbon, each 12″ long.

Assembly

1. **Iron on interfacing**. Follow the instructions for either fast2fuse or fusible interfacing on page 7.
2. **Paint numbers**. Using the diagram below as a guide, paint or embroider numbers on the page face.

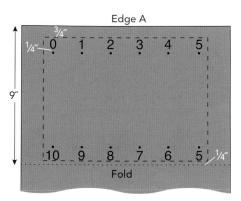

3. **Poke holes in fabric**. About ¼″ below each top number and ¼″ above each bottom number, poke a hole through the fabric and interfacing with a big needle, nail, or awl.

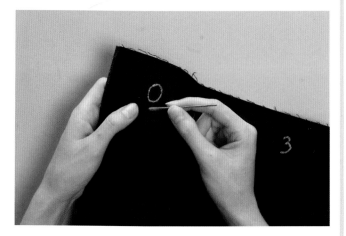

4. **Prepare ribbon**. Knot one end of a length of ribbon; then thread the ribbon through the holes of a button to attach the button. Working from the wrong side of the fabric, insert the ribbon through one of the holes in the fabric to the front of the page face.

Securing the ribbon

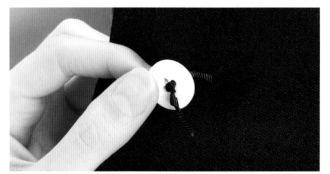

The button works as a washer and keeps the knot from pulling through the hole in the fabric.

 TIP   Use a wide-eyed needle to thread ribbon through a page face.

5. **Thread beads**. Thread 10 beads onto the ribbon. Insert the ribbon through the corresponding hole to form a straight line between 2 numbers.

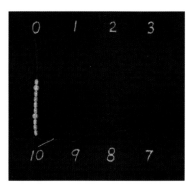

Use enough ribbon to reach between the numbers without pulling the fabric, but not so much that the ribbon sags.

TIP Small children care as much about the color and shape of the beads as they do about the counting, so make sure you pick beads to interest them. My two year old is not as interested in counting as in sliding the little beads up and down the ribbons.

6. **Secure end of ribbon**. Double wrap the ribbon through another button and then knot the ribbon. Trim any excess.

7. **Repeat**. Repeat Steps 4–6 to complete all 6 columns of beads.

8. **Finish page**. Follow the Completing the Page instructions (page 61) to finish the page.

TIP Teach colors by asking the child to find different colored beads. Help children recognize letters by using alphabet beads.

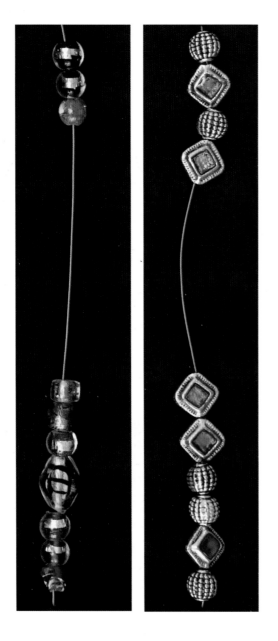

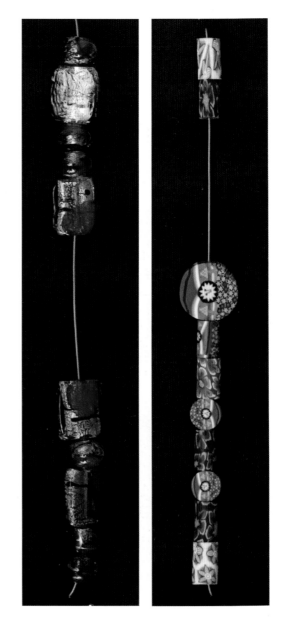

Wallet

My kids were constantly snooping through their dad's wallet. It drove me crazy that he'd let them pull out all the credit cards and ATM cards to play with, so I created a wallet page as a substitute. They still love pulling everything out—but I no longer have to worry about losing things and getting stuck with the credit card bill from someone else's glamorous vacation.

Official Stinky Feet Fan Club Membership Card

Grandparent ID Card

Rebels, Bounty Hunters and Empire Alliance Membership ID valid at any Diplomatic Delegation Meeting

What You'll Need

- Man's shirt or ½ yard of cotton shirting
- Seat of an old pair of jeans
- ¼ yard of regular fusible interfacing
- Thread
- Wallet
- Photos, identification cards, and so on

 The fabrics for this page are particularly personal because you can steal them right out of the closet. I used my husband's old jeans and dress shirt with fraying edges, so my kids are still pickpocketing the same pocket they used to.

How-To

Cutting

- Cut a 15″ × 15″ square of shirting.
- Cut a 15″ × 9½″ rectangle from the seat of a pair of jeans.
- Cut interfacing per the instructions on page 7.

As long as a jeans pocket is accessible, it doesn't matter how the pocket is tilted or what other parts are included. Position the jeans fabric so that there is at least a ½″ seam allowance outside of a pocket edge or the bulky back yoke seam.

 Lay out a pair of old jeans and look for a fabric rectangle that is 15″ wide and 9½″ tall with at least one back pocket accessible. First make a rough cut to get rid of enough of the jeans so that you can easily work with the seat of the pants.

 The back of an old shirt is usually enough to get a 15″ × 15″ square.

Assembly

1. **Iron on interfacing.** Follow the instructions for fusible interfacing on page 7. Remember that the denim part is the page face and should have the big rectangle of interfacing attached to its wrong side. The narrow strip of interfacing will go on the wrong side of the shirting at Edge B.

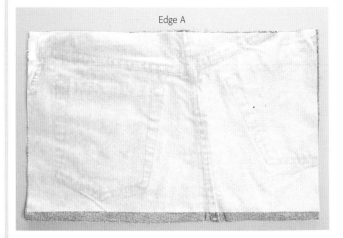

Edge A

2. **Attach shirting to jeans.** With right sides together, pin the shirting square and jeans rectangle together at the bottom edge of the jeans piece. Stitch with a ½″ seam allowance. Press the seam allowance toward the shirting.

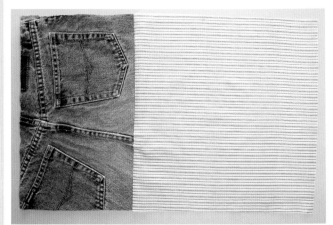

 If there are denim seams that are bulky and difficult to iron, trim the seams to remove the bulk. Remove labels or belt loops that might make seams too thick.

TIP

If you don't want to make cards, you can collect small photos, ticket stubs, fake credit cards that come in the mail, old library cards, real or fake money, and magazine cutouts of favorite things.

TIP
To sew seams with multiple layers of denim, you may want to try a denim (100/16) needle.

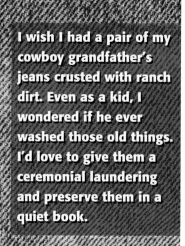

I wish I had a pair of my cowboy grandfather's jeans crusted with ranch dirt. Even as a kid, I wondered if he ever washed those old things. I'd love to give them a ceremonial laundering and preserve them in a quiet book.

3. **Finish page**. Follow the Completing the Page instructions (page 61) to finish the page.

4. **Stock pocket**. Make or collect some identification cards and other paraphernalia to stock the wallet.

TIP
Get a cheap wallet from a dollar store or thrift store. Even better, buy a new one for your favorite guy and use his old one in the quiet book.

TIP
Print personalized identification cards on cardstock. I like to make simple cards with little tidbits about the children. A detailed identification card is a good way to remember statistics about a child at a certain age.

Pocket Purse and Magic Wallet

A woman's purse is a place of secrets and mystery.
Include a little contraband in this purse to keep up
tradition. I keep this page stocked with personalized
"driver's licenses," grandparent identification cards,
photos, money, and an occasional stick of gum.

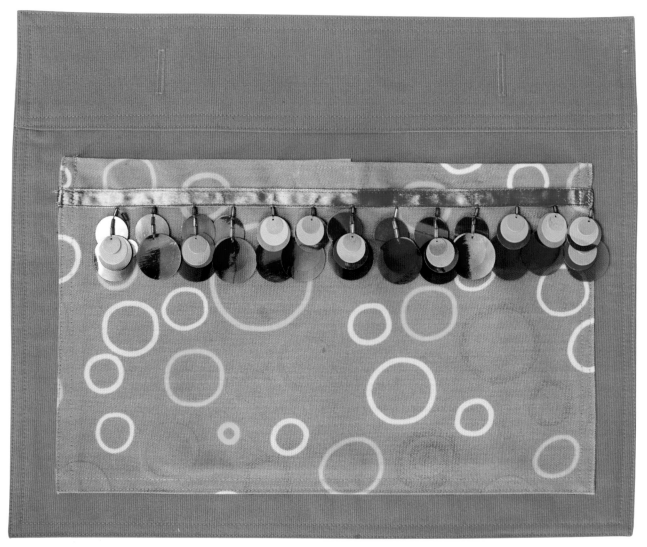

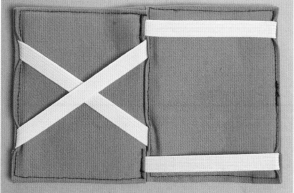

What You'll Need

- ½ yard of bottom-weight fabric for background and Magic Wallet
- ⅓ yard of bottom-weight cotton for Pocket Purse
- ¼ yard of regular fusible interfacing or fast2fuse *(If using fast2fuse, you also need a 2½" × 15" strip of regular fusible interfacing.)*
- 1" piece of ¾"-wide sew-in hook-and-loop tape
- ½ yard of ½" elastic for Magic Wallet
- Small piece (3½" × 5") of fast2fuse for Magic Wallet
- Thread
- Stuff to go in the purse
- *Optional: ¼ yard of a different bottom-weight fabric for Magic Wallet*
- *Optional: 14" of decorative froufrou*

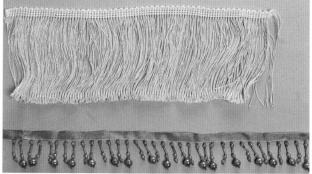

Pick froufrou with both color and texture appeal.

How-To

Cutting

- Cut a 23½" × 15" rectangle of background fabric.
- Cut a 9½" × 14" rectangle of Pocket Purse fabric.

- Cut fast2fuse or interfacing per the instructions on page 7.
- Cut 4 rectangles 4" × 5" of pocket fabric for Magic Wallet
- Cut 2 rectangles 3½" × 2½" of fast2fuse for Magic Wallet.
- Cut 2 strips 4¼" long of ½" elastic for Magic Wallet.
- Cut 2 strips 3½" long of ½" elastic for Magic Wallet.

Assembly

1. **Iron on interfacing.** Follow the instructions for either fast2fuse or fusible interfacing on page 7.

2. **Make Pocket Purse.** Using the 9½" × 14" rectangle, follow the directions on pages 7–8 to make a pocket, using a 9½" edge as the top of the pocket.

   Pin and then stitch the bristly side of the 1" piece of hook-and-loop tape to the center of the pocket top edge.

Optional: Topstitch froufrou along the top edge of the pocket to cover the stitching of the pocket top. Tuck the ends of the froufrou to the back of the pocket.

3. **Attach Pocket Purse**. Position and pin the pocket on the page face to mark where to attach the soft side of the 1″ hook-and-loop tape. (Do not pin the top half of the pocket to the page face; leave it loose to mark.) Pin the hook-and-loop tape into place and stitch it down.

4. Finish pinning around the edges of the pocket. Edgestitch and double stitch the side and bottom edges of the pocket.

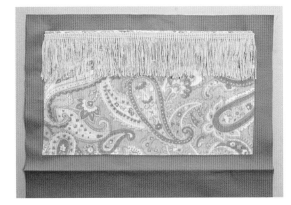

5. **Finish page**. Follow the Completing the Page instructions (page 61) to finish the page.

6. **Stock Pocket Purse with fun stuff**.

My grandmother was extraordinarily proper, but because she was diabetic and had to keep her blood sugar level stable, occasional breaches in etiquette occurred. Little caramel cubes with crackling wrappers still remind me of her. She thought she was so sneaky, and I loved getting a bit of candy in church.

 Instead of making a Magic Wallet, you can use any little purse or wallet you find in the back of your drawer or in the toy department.

Magic Wallet

For the wallet, you will use the 4 rectangles of Magic Wallet fabric, the 2 fast2fuse rectangles, and the elastic strips.

1. Press ½″ down along all 4 edges of all 4 rectangles. Stitch the 2 strips of 4¼″ elastic to the *long edge* of the *wrong side* of 1 rectangle, with the ends about ½″ from the top and bottom, so the free ends form an **X**.

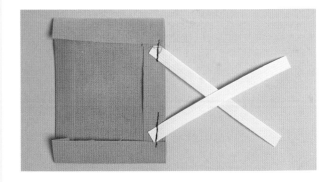

2. Flip the rectangle with the elastic **X** over so the right side is facing up. Stitch the free ends of the elastic **X** to the wrong side of another rectangle.

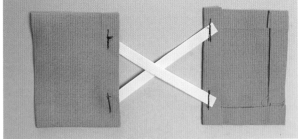

Make sure the right side of 1 rectangle is facing up and the right side of the other is facing down.

3. Almost at the top and bottom edges of the rectangle, stitch the 3½″ elastic pieces perpendicular to the long edge of the wrong side of 1 rectangle.

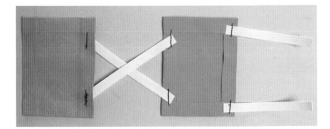

4. Following the manufacturer's instructions, fuse a $3\frac{1}{2}'' \times 2\frac{1}{2}''$ rectangle of fast2fuse inside the pressed edges of each of the 2 free rectangles.

This stiffened rectangle will cover the ends of the elastic strips.

5. With wrong sides together, edgestitch all 4 sides of the stiffened rectangle to the rectangle with the 4 elastic strips. With wrong sides together, edgestitch only 3 sides of the rectangle with the elastic **X**; secure the top, the bottom, and the edge with the elastic **X**, but leave the fourth side open.

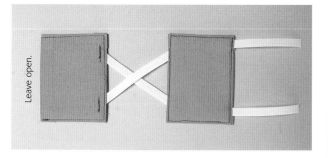

Leave open.

6. Fold the rectangles so the elastic **X** overlaps 1 rectangle and the perpendicular elastics are free.

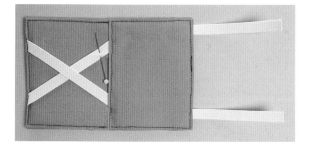

7. Fold the perpendicular elastics back over the rectangle toward the elastic **X** and pin in place.

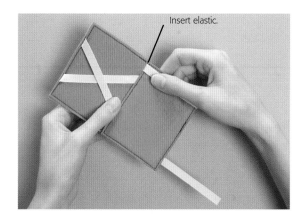

Insert elastic.

8. Stitch the perpendicular elastics to the open edge of the opposite rectangle. Make sure not to catch the elastic **X** in the stitching.

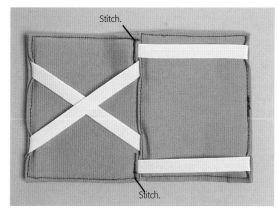

Stitch.

Stitch.

If the elastic got tangled while you were stitching the open side closed, rearrange the elastic to match the picture.

9. Edgestitch the fourth side of the rectangle closed. Be careful not to catch any of the elastic in the stitching.

10. Stick a card or a folded dollar bill on top of the elastic, close the wallet, and open it from the other side. Magic! The card will be tucked safely under the elastic.

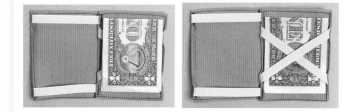

Family Photos

I've always thought of photo albums as propaganda tools. I don't include pictures of my kids fighting or me losing my temper, and I like for the kids to imagine that these things never happen. According to our scrapbook history, they don't.

What You'll Need

- ¹/₂ yard of bottom-weight background fabric
- ¹/₄ yard of bottom-weight fabric for book cover
- ¹/₄ yard of regular fusible interfacing
- 3 PhotoFabric sheets or iron-on transfer sheets and cotton fabric suitable to receive the iron-on
- 1″ piece of ³/₄″-wide sew-in hook-and-loop tape
- Thread
- At least 12 digital photos

How-To

Cutting

- Cut a 23¹/₂″ × 15″ rectangle of background fabric.
- Cut interfacing per the instructions on page 7.
- Cut 2 rectangles 5¹/₂″ × 13″ of book cover fabric.
- Cut a 3″ × 5″ rectangle of book cover fabric for closure tab.

Assembly

1. **Organize digital photos**. Select 12 photos (or photo groups) you would like to use. In a word-processing or photo-editing program (I use Microsoft Word), go to Page Setup and set the paper orientation to land-scape. The page is divided into 4 equal quadrants—in half top to bottom and in half left to right. Use 3 pages of 4 quadrants each to include a total of 12 pages in your book. Copy and paste your photos into the 4 quadrants on each of the 3 pages. Leave ¹/₂″ margins on all 4 sides of each photo quadrant for seam allowances.

You will need 3 pages like this to create a total of 12 pages in the album.

TIP You can use more than 1 photo per page as long as you don't exceed the maximum dimensions of 4¹/₂″ wide by 3¹/₄″ tall per quadrant.

PAGE 1	
2	11
12	1
PAGE 2	
4	9
10	3
PAGE 3	
6	7
8	5

Four quadrants per page—landscape orientation

If you want your photos in a particular order, decide that order now and number your photos from 1–12.

This chart can help you group your photos so that they will be in the correct order once the book is printed, sewn, and folded.

2. **Print photos**. Print all 3 pages of photos to the PhotoFabric sheets and make them colorfast according to the manufacturer's instructions, or print them on the iron-on transfer sheets following the manufacturer's directions (remember to protect the iron-on). Press each sheet flat.

3. **Cut photo pages**. Cut the printed fabric sheets in half lengthwise to form strips with 2 photo pages on each strip.

TIP Consider different themes for your book. You can select photos from one year of a child's life. Or try a color book, matching the child's clothing with other objects of the same color. It's easy to add words to personalize the book. Focus on animals, emotions, or any theme.

4. Stitch pages. With right sides together, pin appropriate pages together. Using ¼″ seam allowances, stitch the pages together on 2 long sides and a short side.

Trim the corners. Turn the pages right side out. Poke out the corners. Press the 3 stitched edges and turn under ¼″ on the raw edges of the open end. Edgestitch all 4 sides.

5. Make book cover. With right sides together, pin the 2 rectangles of cover fabric together. With ½″ seam allowances, stitch the rectangles together along 2 long sides and a short side.

Trim the corners and turn the cover right side out. Poke out the corners. Press the 3 stitched edges and turn under ¼″ on the raw edges of the open end. Edgestitch along the open side to close the page. Edgestitch ¼″ from the edge around the remaining 3 sides.

6. Make hook-and-loop tape tab. With right sides together, fold the 3″ × 5″ rectangle in half lengthwise and, using a ¼″ seam allowance, stitch the long sides

and a short side closed. Trim the corners and turn the tab right side out. Poke out the corners. Press the edges flat.

7. Attach hook-and-loop tape. The soft side of the hook-and-loop tape goes on the book, and the bristly side goes on the tab. Sew the 1″ strip of the bristly side to the finished end of the tab, leaving the raw end of the tab free. Sew a 1″ strip of the soft side of the hook-and-loop tape to the outside of the book cover, halfway down the short side of the cover and aligned with the edgestitching.

8. Insert pages. With photo pages in the correct order and neatly stacked, center the stack of photo pages on the book cover.

Mark the center of the pages—this is the center seam of the book. Matching the bobbin thread to the book cover color and the top thread to the photo page color, stitch through all layers to secure the pages to the cover at the center seam of the book.

Stitch through all layers again ¼″ from both sides of the center seam, making 3 parallel lines in the middle of the pages.

These 3 lines form the spine of the book and help the pages to lie flat.

TIP

Getting a pin through all those thicknesses can be difficult, so I hold the pages in place and stitch without pinning. To prevent the pages from shifting, you can clip them in place with a binder clip from your office supplies.

9. **Position closure tab**. Use the hook-and-loop tape to fasten the tab to the front cover of the book. Position the raw end of the tab on the back cover of the book and pin it in place. Open the hook-and-loop tape end of the tab from the front cover of the book.

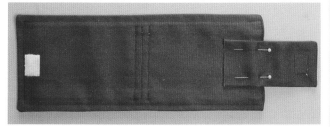

Do not sew the tab in place yet. It will be sewn in when the book is attached to the page face.

10. **Iron on interfacing**. Follow the instructions for fusible interfacing on page 7.

11. **Attach book to page face**. With the book closed, center the book on the page face. Keeping the book positioned, open it and turn all the pages to the left, then pin the back cover to the page face. Make sure to move the pins holding the tab in place to the outside so you can remove them after stitching the book in place.

   Following the edgestitching already on the back cover, stitch the back half of the book's cover to the page face along the 3 outer edges and then along the edge of the last photo page. Reinforce the stitching over the tab.

12. **Finish page**. Follow the Completing the Page instructions (page 61) to finish the page.

TIP

Choose photos that children like, not just ones you like. I am always tempted to use only photos in which we look like respectable people. My kids love the candid and silly shots.

TIP

You can pick a busy pattern for the background fabric because it won't compete with the activity on this page.

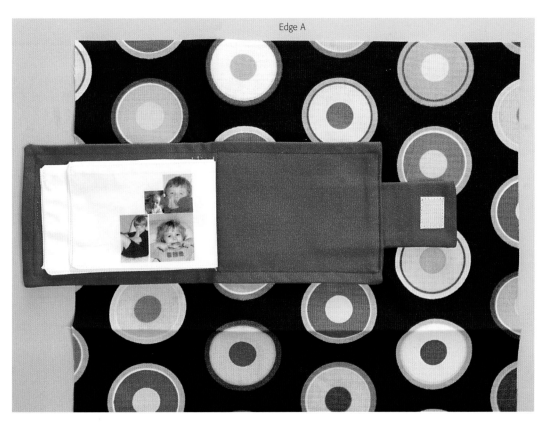

Edge A

Family Tree

Between the leaves of this tree are several generations
of family. Even though my kids haven't met most of
these ancestors, they know their faces.

What You'll Need

- ■ ½ yard of green bottom-weight fabric for background and leaves
- ■ ¼ yard of brown fabric for trunk
- ■ ¼ yard of regular fusible interfacing
- ■ ¼ yard of double-sided fusible web
- ■ Brown thread
- ■ Green thread
- ■ 7 digital family photos
- ■ PhotoFabric sheets, or iron-on transfer sheets and cotton fabric suitable to receive the iron-ons

How-To

Cutting

- ■ Cut a 23½″ × 15″ rectangle of green background fabric. With right sides together, fold the remaining green fabric in half and use the pattern on page 31 to cut 6 pairs of leaf shapes.
- ■ Cut interfacing per the instructions on page 7.

Assembly

1. Select photos. Find 7 digital photos of family members or family groups.

Organization Options

- ■ Use the child's face for the main picture, her parents above her, and her grandparents in the branches.
- ■ Using a picture of the family rather than an individual in the main picture allows you to add another generation in the top branches.
- ■ Ignore genetic lineage altogether and simply hide random family members in the branches. Kids aren't looking for pedigree chart exactness—you can randomly assign favorite cousins, aunts, families, or grandparents a spot behind any leaf.

2. Size digital photos. Crop or shrink the photos down to approximately 2½″ × 4″ for the main photo and 2½″ × 2½″ for the leaf photos.

TIP Use close-ups. Photos with small figures or too much action can be hard to see.

3. Prepare photos. With photos this small, you can group several on a single page to print—just leave at least 1″ between photos for borders. Following the manufacturer's instructions, print the photos to PhotoFabric sheets or iron-on transfer sheets.

For PhotoFabric, trim each photo leave a ½″ border around all 4 sides, and press the border to the back of each photo.

4. Iron on interfacing. Follow the instructions for fusible interfacing on page 7.

5. Make leaf flaps. With right sides together, pin 2 leaf shapes together. Using a ¼" seam allowance, stitch around the leaf-shaped sides but not the straight edge at the top.

Clip the curves and trim the seam allowances. Turn the leaf right side out and poke out the corners and curves. Press the edges. Repeat for a total of 6 leaves.

Stitch, trim, and turn each leaf right side out. Repeat until you have 6 leaves.

 TIP Don't worry that the leaves are not all exactly alike; the organic nature of this design makes slight variation an asset.

6. Make tree trunk. Following the manufacturer's instructions, fuse the double-sided fusible web to the wrong side of the brown tree trunk fabric. Enlarge the pattern on page 31 to 200% and cut a tree trunk shape from the fusible-backed fabric.

 TIP Use parchment paper or a pressing sheet to protect the side of the fusible web that you are not yet ready to use.

Position and pin the tree trunk so the bottom of the trunk is at the bottom of the page face. Following the manufacturer's instructions, fuse the trunk to the bottom of the page face.

Set your sewing machine to zigzag at a minimal stitch length and medium width. Zigzag around the raw edges of the trunk. Don't worry if the zigzagging isn't perfect. Remember, it's a tree; all trees are crooked.

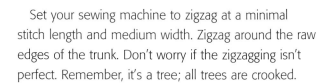

Edge A

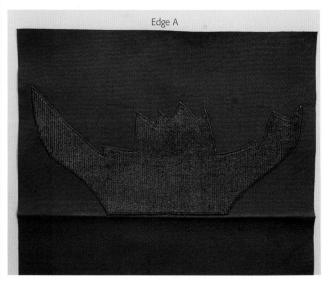

 TIP You can easily identify the bottom of the page face by folding the background fabric along the edge of the interfacing you have fused to the back.

7. Attach first 3 photos. Position the main trunk photo and the first pair of branch photos on the page as shown. Topstitch each photo (or fuse iron-on photos) into place.

8. Attach first pair of leaf flaps. Cut 1″ off the straight top edge of 2 leaves to shorten them.

Position the first row of leaves so the straight edge is ¼″ above the photo and the leaf points up. Use a ¼″ seam allowance to stitch the leaf edge parallel to the top of the photo.

Fold and press the leaf down so that it covers the photo. Using a ⅜″ seam allowance from the folded-down edge, edgestitch the leaf to complete the flap. Repeat for the other leaf flap in the first row of leaves.

9. Attach 4 remaining photos. Position the top row of photos on the page. Topstitch each photo (or fuse iron-on photos) into place.

10. Baste top leaves in place. Position 4 leaves, pointing down to cover the top 4 photos, and pin the tops of the leaves in place to cover the photos. If a leaf's top edge is uneven, trim the excess from the top so the raw edges are even with the raw edge of the top of the page. Baste the row of leaves in place with a ¼" seam allowance.

11. Pin the side leaf flaps toward the center of the page so they don't get caught when you sew the page side seams.

12. Finish page. Follow the Completing the Page instructions (page 61) to finish the page. The top edges of the leaves are sewn inside the page.

The bottoms of these leaves should overlap the tops of the bottom row.

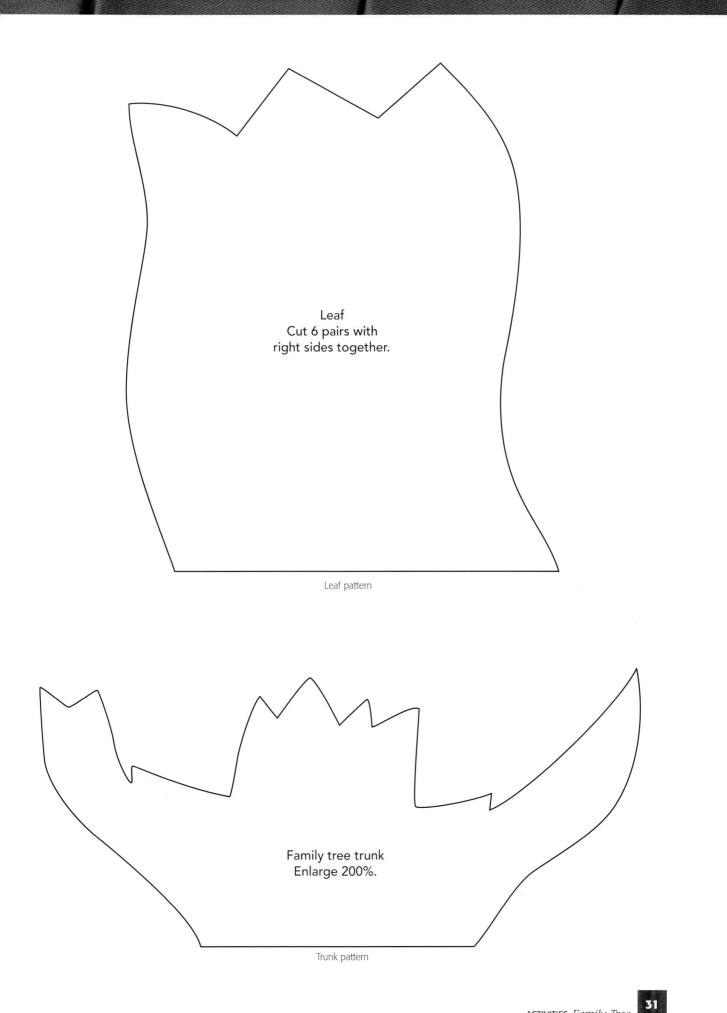

Leaf
Cut 6 pairs with
right sides together.

Leaf pattern

Family tree trunk
Enlarge 200%.

Trunk pattern

Magnifying Glass

The magnifier provides a great scope to play the "Can you find a…?" game. Make a collage of a child's favorite things. Include photos and activities specific to the child's age and tastes.

What You'll Need

- ½ yard of bottom-weight background fabric
- ¼ yard of fast2fuse (suggested) or regular fusible interfacing *(If using fast2fuse, you also need a 2½" × 15" strip of regular fusible interfacing.)*
- 1 yard of ribbon, 1" or less in width
- Magnifying glass
- Trinkets and buttons
- Thread
- *Optional: PhotoFabric sheet, or iron-on transfer sheet and cotton fabric suitable to receive the iron-on*

How-To

Cutting

- Cut a 23½" × 15" rectangle of background fabric.
- Cut a rectangle of background fabric 3" wider and 3" longer than your magnifying glass, with a maximum length of 10", for the pocket.
- Cut fast2fuse or interfacing per the instructions on page 7.

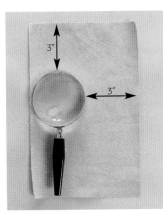

Assembly

1. **Iron on interfacing**. Follow the instructions for fast2fuse or fusible interfacing on page 7.
2. **Make pocket for magnifying glass**. Follow the instructions on page 8 to make the pocket.
3. **Attach ribbon leash**. Fold over one end of the ribbon and pin it to the inside of the pocket side edge so the folded end will be caught in the stitching when you attach the pocket.

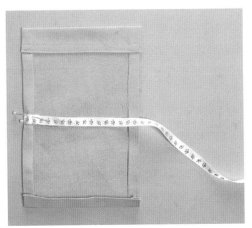

The long end of the ribbon is free.

4. **Attach pocket**. Center the pocket on the back of the page with the bottom of the pocket just above the fold line of the page face. Pin the pocket in place. Edgestitch and double stitch around the sides and bottom of the pocket. Be sure to keep the long end of the ribbon free.

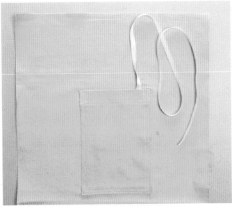

Stitch the pocket to the back of the page, with the top of the pocket toward the thin strip of interfacing.

5. **Attach embellishments**. Sew buttons and trinkets to the page face as desired.

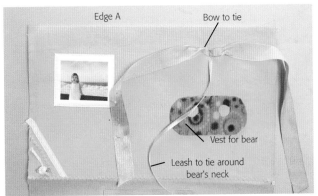

Machine stitch what you can before you hand stitch the rest.

Settle into a comfy chair and call a chatty friend or put in a movie, because hand stitching these buttons and trinkets can take a while.

 Clean your ears before giving this page to children because inevitably they finish looking at the buttons and turn the magnifying glass to you.

Follow the bead-stringing instructions on pages 13–14 to add some name beads.

6. **Finish page**. Follow the Completing the Page instructions (page 61) to finish the page; then tie the free end of the ribbon to the magnifying glass and insert it into the pocket.

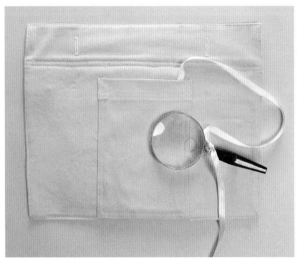

The back of the page.

When I found out I would be having a daughter, I swore she would never wear pink. I was positive that our culture conditions little girls to love pink and froufrou. My husband always countered that our daughter would not be the site of my cultural revolution, and if she wanted pink, she would have it.

Well, despite my best efforts, I have a little girl who wears only pink, who gets out of bed and puts her shoes, purse, and jewelry on before she gets her diaper changed, and who insists on wearing a pink feather boa to the grocery store.

And, of course, we celebrate her in all of her pinkness.

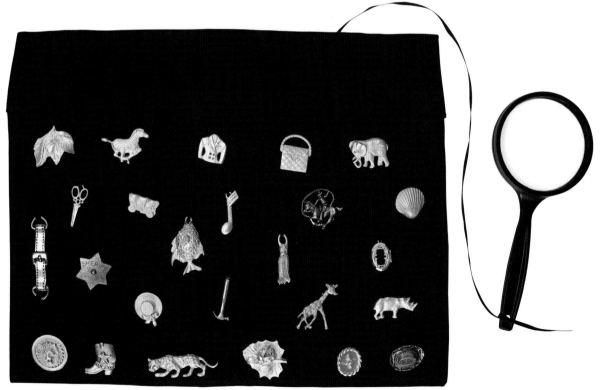

Another idea, just use a bunch of fun buttons!

Trinket Pocket Variation

Instead of sewing all the little trinkets to the page, you can use the page as a pocket and fill it up with trinkets.

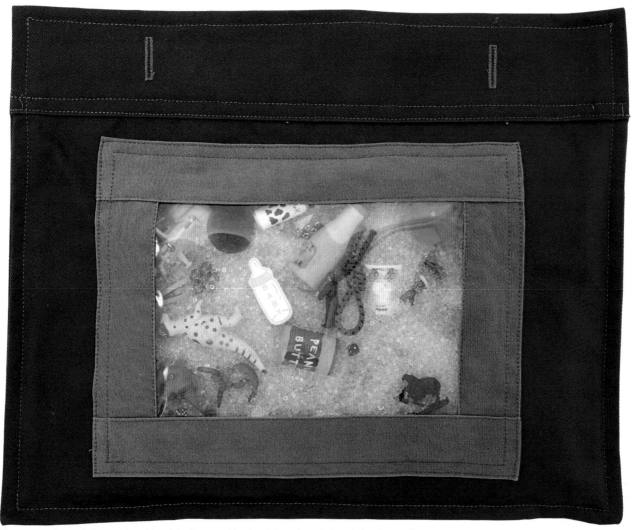

The squeeze-bag variation can be a bit noisier, but searching for trinkets through the window is great fun.

Instead of making a pocket for a magnifying glass, put a card in the pocket either listing or showing a picture of all the trinkets to be found in the window. Regular fusible interfacing works best for this variation because the page needs to be bent and manipulated.

1. Before you put the page together, stitch a rectangle of Quilter's Vinyl (see Sources, page 63) to the page face. Double stitch around the vinyl window and then cut out the fabric behind the window. (For nicer edges, frame the Quilter's Vinyl with fabric before stitching it to the page face.) Attach the card pocket to the back of the page (see page 8)

2. Once the window is complete, fill the window pocket with trinkets and some filler material like rice or beads. Follow the Completing the Page instructions (page 61) to sew the bag shut.

Matching Pockets

Use this design for matching flowers, sports, holidays, or
any themed pairs. Kids love to play with the animals,
touch the various fur fabrics, and tuck the buttons into
the matching fabric pocket. Colors are simple and easy
for little ones to identify and match.

What You'll Need

- ½ yard of bottom-weight background fabric
- Scraps (at least 3" × 3½") of 6 different fabrics to match button pairs
- ¼ yard of fast2fuse or regular fusible interfacing *(If using fast2fuse, you also need a 2½" × 15" strip of regular fusible interfacing.)*
- 2 yards of thin ribbon or cord
- 6 pairs of matching buttons
- Thread

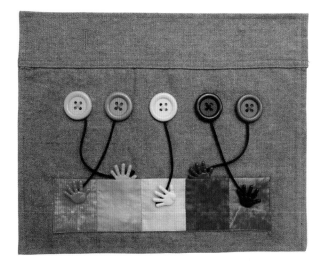

TIP Sometimes free fabric swatches are big enough to make the pockets. If you can get a 3" × 3½" swatch, you have enough for a pocket. Also check precut flat folds for bargain prices.

How-To

Cutting

- Cut a 23½" × 15" rectangle of background fabric.
- Cut a 13" × 3½" backing panel for the pockets from the background fabric (or 11" × 3½" if you're making only 5 pockets)
- Cut fast2fuse or interfacing per the instructions on page 7.
- Cut 6 pocket rectangles of scrap fabric, each 3" wide × 3½" high (or 5 rectangles if you're making only 5 pockets)

- You'll need a 10" length of ribbon or cord for each button pair, but don't trim it to size yet, because the ends might fray before you're ready to use it.

Assembly

1. **Iron on interfacing**. Follow the instructions for either fast2fuse or fusible interfacing on page 7.

2. **Plan your design**. Decide the order for the pockets on the bottom row first. To avoid confusion, try to split up fabrics that are similar.

Arrange fabrics for the pockets first.

Next arrange the buttons on the top row. Consider how complicated you want the activity to be. For small children, I like to make it very simple by keeping the button on the top row close to its matching pocket in the second row. You may want to write out your plan on a chart you can refer to later.

Arrange the buttons on the top row in a different color order than the pocket fabrics.

3. Make pockets. With right sides together and using $1/2$" seam allowances, stitch together the long edges of the little pocket rectangles to form 1 long pieced rectangle. Press seams to one side.

With right sides together and using $1/2$" seam allowances, stitch the pieced rectangle to the backing rectangle on 3 sides, leaving a short side open. Clip the corners of the stitched short side.

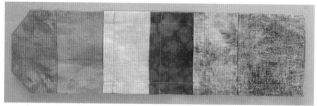

Turn the pocket right side out and press the seams.

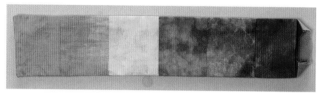

At the open end, turn $1/2$" of fabric to the inside of the page and press. Press the ends in but don't stitch the page closed yet.

4. Attach pockets. Center the pocket rectangle on the background fabric 1" above the fold that forms the bottom edge of the page face. Pin in place.

Edgestitch around the 2 sides and the bottom of the entire rectangle to form a wide pocket; then stitch in the seam lines to divide the pockets.

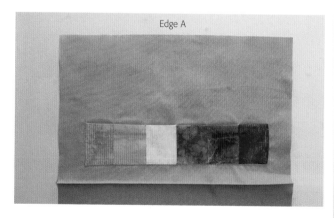

Edge A

TIP

If you're fussy about thread color, use invisible thread or change thread to match each pocket; otherwise, stitch all the pockets in a neutral color.

5. Attach bottom buttons and ribbon. Use a 10" length of ribbon or cord for each button pair. Tie a knot at one end of each cord. Attach the ribbon to the button that will go into the pocket. Repeat to attach ribbon to the rest of the buttons that go into the pockets.

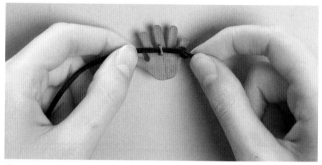

If your buttons have big shanks on the back, you can thread the ribbon into the button shank and the knot will hold the button.

If your buttons have holes or small shanks, you'll likely have to hand stitch them to the ribbon at or above a knot.

6. Attach top buttons and ribbon. Mark a dot centered above each pocket and 2" below the top edge of the page face to guide your placement of the top buttons.

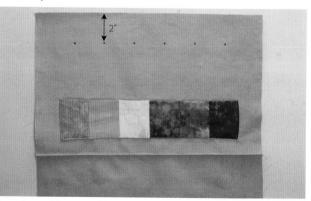

These dots will be covered by the buttons, so don't worry about leaving the marks.

Refer to your chart for the correct order in which to position the top buttons. Pin the loose end of the ribbon where the top button will be. Stitch the ribbon to the page face. Machine stitch well over the ribbon so it won't pull loose.

Trim the ribbon below the knot at the bottom button and above the stitching of the top row.

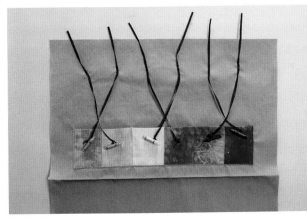

Leave enough ribbon for the bottom button to reach but not so much that the ribbon sags.

7. **Sew buttons**. Sew the top row of buttons securely to the page face at the top end of the corresponding buttons, covering the end of the ribbons.

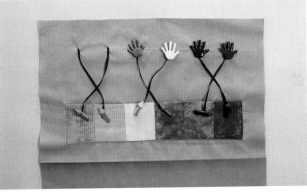

Double check that the pairs are matched and that the ribbons reach the appropriate pockets.

8. **Finish page**. Follow the Completing the Page instructions (page 61) to finish the page.

A printed strip works just as well.

If you can't find a fabric print you need, consider making your own using a print-to-fabric sheet.

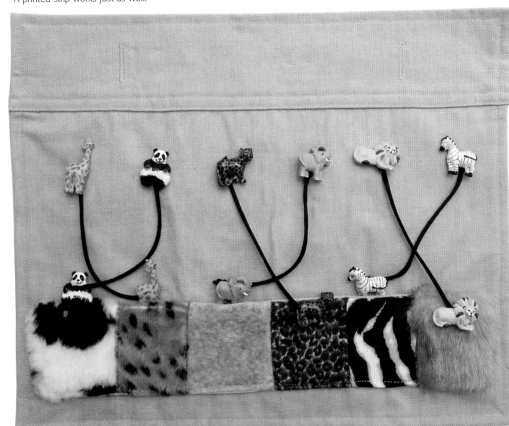

If using fake fur, choose a low-pile fabric on one end. You will be leaving that end open and then pressing and folding in the raw edges to stitch them closed—ironing a furry fabric is nearly impossible.

Dress-Up Doll

Buttoning, buckling, and tying are more fun on a familiar figure… although I must admit that we spend more time weaving crazy patterns with the shoelaces than actually tying them. I'm hoping my kids learn to tie their shoes sometime before they leave for college.

What You'll Need

- ½ yard of bottom-weight background fabric
- ¼ yard of fast2fuse or regular fusible interfacing
  (*If using fast2fuse, you also need a 2½" × 15" strip of regular fusible interfacing.*)
- 8" × 10" close-up digital photograph (A school photo is perfect for this page.)
- ¼ yard of bottom-weight fabric for pants
- ¼ yard of fleece for sweatshirt
- ¼ yard of fabric-backed vinyl or heavy fabric for shoes
- Scraps or ⅛ yard of flesh-colored cotton for hands
- PhotoFabric sheet, or iron-on transfer sheet and cotton fabric suitable to receive the iron-on
- Shoelaces, 18" to 24" long
- Large (about ⅞") button
- Narrow, lightweight belt with buckle
- Thread
- *Optional: Eyelets*

How-To

Cutting

- Cut a 15" × 23½" rectangle of background fabric.
- Cut the fast2fuse or fusible interfacing per the instructions on page 7.
- Using the patterns on pages 44–45 as a guide, fold the fabrics right sides together and cut:
  - 2 pants from bottom-weight fabric
  - 2 of each sweatshirt side from fleece
  - 4 shoes from vinyl
  - 4 hands from flesh-colored cotton

Assembly

1. **Iron on interfacing**. Follow the instructions for fast2fuse or fusible interfacing on page 7.

2. **Digitize and transfer photo**. Scan and print the 8" × 10" close-up photo to either a PhotoFabric sheet or an iron-on transfer sheet. Trim around the edges of the photo if necessary.

If using PhotoFabric, press under ¼" on all 4 sides of the photo and then position the photo sideways and centered 1" from the top and from one side edge of the page face. Pin and edgestitch into place.

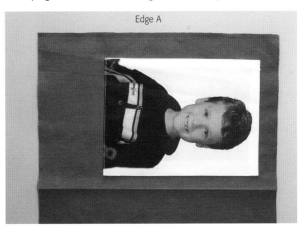

Edge A

3. **Make hands and sweatshirt**. With right sides together, use a ¼" seam allowance to stitch together 2 hand shapes around the rounded edges but not the wrist. Trim seams, clip curves, and turn right side out. Press the edges. Repeat for the second hand.

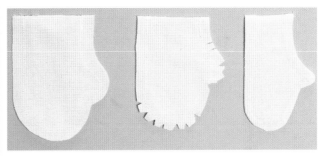

Pin a hand in place on the wrong side of one of the sweatshirt sleeves. With wrong sides together, pin 2 sweatshirts together so the hand is sandwiched between the 2 layers.

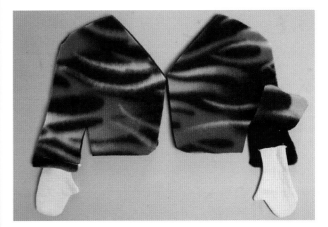

Edgestitch the fleece together, securing the hand in place. Repeat for the second hand and sweatshirt.

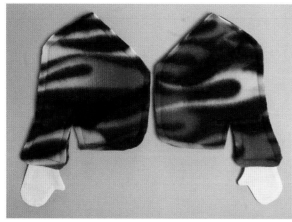

The raw edges of the fleece will be exposed in the seam.

Mark the location of the buttonhole on one side of the sweatshirt and sew the buttonhole. Sew a button to the other side of the sweatshirt.

 TIP Add hair bows, jewelry, rings, or other accessories to personalize your little figure.

4. Make pants and shoes. With right sides together, use ¼″ seam allowances to stitch the pants pieces together along the side seams, bottoms, and inseams, leaving the waist open. Trim corners, clip curves, and turn right side out. Press under ½″ around the top of the waistline and pin the waist closed.

The waist of the pants remains open to turn them right side out.

The vinyl doesn't fray, so a quick and easy way to sew the shoes is to sew them wrong sides together with ¼″ seam allowances. No clipping and turning necessary!

Option: With right sides together, use ¼″ seam allowances to stitch both pairs of shoes along the sides and bottom. Trim seams, clip curves, and turn right side out.

Stitch the open top of the shoes to the bottom of the pants so the shoes are behind the finished edge of the pants.

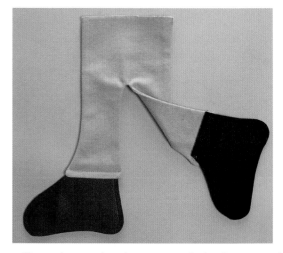

Affix eyelets to the shoes or cut holes big enough to thread a shoelace through. Insert the laces.

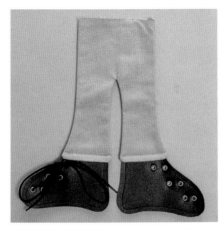

5. Attach pants to photo. Pin the pants in place on the photo. Edgestitch the waist of the pants to attach them and close the waist.

 Don't worry that the pants are not at the natural waist. The design is purposefully distorted, and the sweatshirt helps cover the shirt in the photo.

6. Attach belt. Center the buckle, cut off the excess belt length, and stitch the sides of the belt to the sides of the pants.

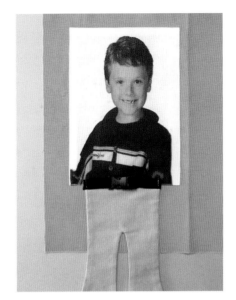

7. Attach sweatshirt. Button the sweatshirt closed and pin in place. Edgestitch the shoulders and side seams of the sweatshirt to the page but let the arms hang loose.

8. Finish page. Follow the Completing the Page instructions (page 61) to finish the page.

 Pin the hanging pieces to the center of the page so they don't get caught in the side seams.

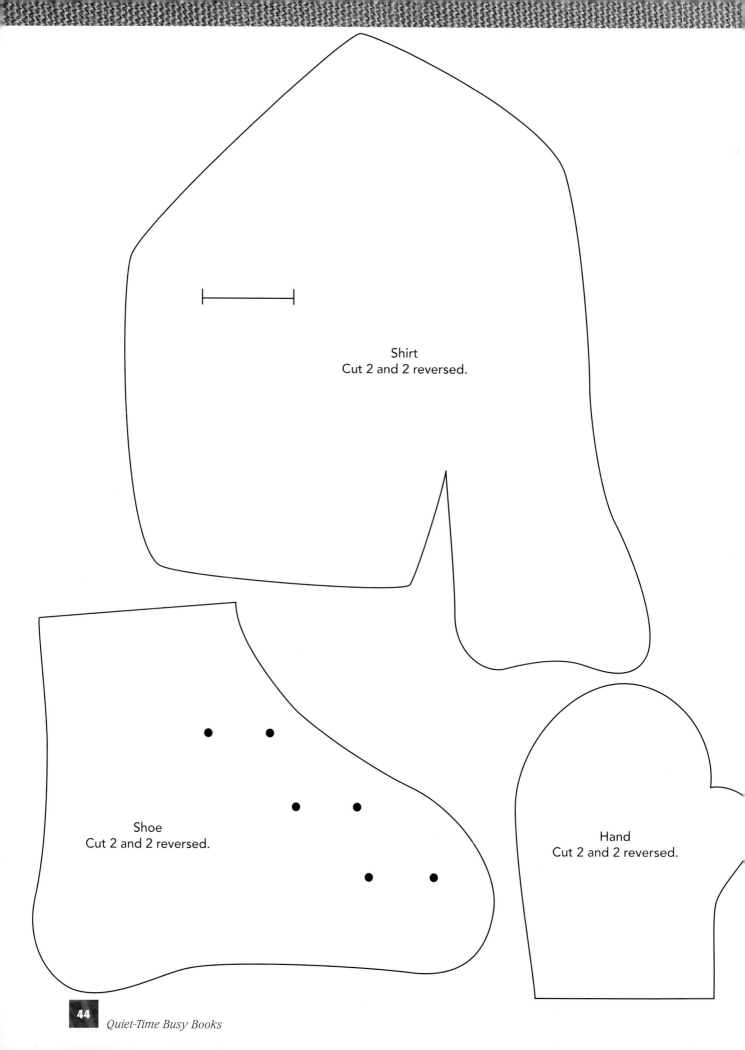

Shirt
Cut 2 and 2 reversed.

Shoe
Cut 2 and 2 reversed.

Hand
Cut 2 and 2 reversed.

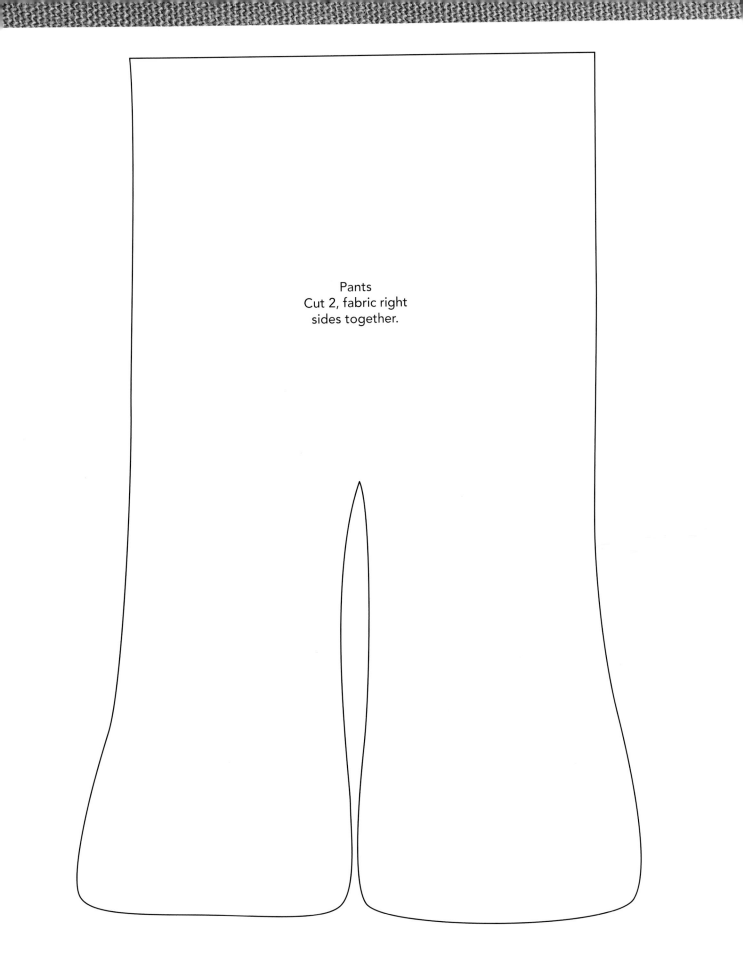

Pants
Cut 2, fabric right
sides together.

Peek-a-Boo Mittens

This page activity is simple enough that the background fabric can be busy. The border fabric is a great opportunity to preserve a scrap of a favorite shirt. If the child has grown out of the shirt in the photo—or stained the front beyond anyone's interest in it as a hand-me-down—use it for the border.

What You'll Need

- ½ yard of bottom-weight background fabric
- ⅓ yard of contrasting fabric for border behind photo
- ¼ yard of fast2fuse or regular fusible interfacing
  (*If using fast2fuse, you also need a 2½″ × 14″ strip of regular fusible interfacing.*)
- ¼ yard of fleece
- Digital close-up photo of a face (5″ to 7″ tall and 7″ to 9″ wide)
- Thread
- PhotoFabric sheet, or iron-on transfer sheet and cotton fabric suitable to receive the iron-on

 TIP Some transfer sheets allow you to transfer the iron-on to colored fabric—check to see whether your transfer sheets require a white background before choosing the fabric to receive the transfer.

How-To

Cutting

- Cut a 15″ × 23½″ rectangle of background fabric.
- Cut the fast2fuse or fusible interfacing per the instructions on page 7.
- Cut 4 mittens out of fleece using the enlarged pattern on page 49 as a guide.

Assembly

1. **Iron on interfacing.** Follow the instructions for fast2fuse or fusible interfacing on page 7.

2. **Transfer photo to fabric.** Scan a paper photo or take a digital photo. Resize the photo to print between 4″ and 6″ tall and 6″ and 8″ wide. Transfer the photo to the fabric by means of one of the methods described on page 48.

TIP Choose a photo that is not busy—look for close-ups without background clutter. I like to use a close-up of someone's face so the page mimics the game of peek-a-boo.

3. **Attach photo to page face.** Position the photo so it is centered from the side edges of the page face and at least 1″ down from the top edge of the page. Pin in place. Edgestitch the border to the background fabric.

4. **Make mittens.** With right sides together, stitch 2 mitten pieces together leaving a ½″ seam allowance. Trim seams and clip corners and curves. Turn the mitten right side out. Repeat for the second mitten.

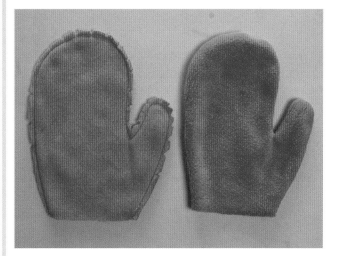

Photo Fabric Sheet

1. **Print photo**. Follow the manufacturer's instructions for printing the photo and making it colorfast.

2. **Trim.** Trim the edges, leaving at least ³/₄″ around the photo—for a wider white border, leave more fabric around the edges.

3. **Press.** With wrong sides together, press under at least ¹/₄″ around all 4 sides of the photo.

4. **Pin.** Cut the border fabric, leaving at least 1¹/₂″ of fabric around all 4 sides of the photo. Center and pin the photo to the border fabric. Edgestitch in place.

Iron-on Transfer Sheets

1. **Print photo.** Follow the manufacturer's instructions to print the photo to the transfer sheet.

2. **Trim.** Trim the transfer sheet to the edges of the photo.

3. **Transfer photo to fabric.** Cut the border fabric, leaving at least 2″ of fabric around the edges to form the fabric border. Center the photo and iron it onto the fabric, following the manufacturer's instructions. Be sure to put a transfer protection sheet between the photo and the ironing board when you press the border edges down, so the photo doesn't melt to the ironing board. Be careful any time you are ironing around the photo, even from the back.

Border

Whether you use an iron-on transfer or a PhotoFabric sheet, treat the border fabric the same.

1. **Trim fabric around photo.** Leave a border that is at least 1″ higher and 1″ wider than your photo. (You can make the border wider, but make sure the total dimensions of the photo and the border are not bigger than 7¹/₂″ high by 10″ wide).

2. **Press.** Press at least ¹/₄″ to the back on all 4 sides of the border fabric.

TIP Because the iron-on can peel around the edges, you may want to zigzag around the edges of the photo. Adjust your stitch length to the lowest setting and width as desired.

5. **Attach mittens**. Position the mittens so they cover the photo when closed. Pin and edgestitch about 4″ along the outer edge of each mitten.

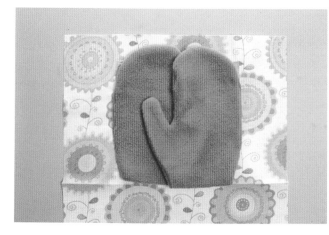

 The mittens look cute if they're a little bit crooked, so don't fuss too much about getting them straight.

6. **Finish page**. Follow the Completing the Page instructions (page 61) to finish the page.

Mitten pattern
Enlarge 200%
Cut 2 and 2 reversed.

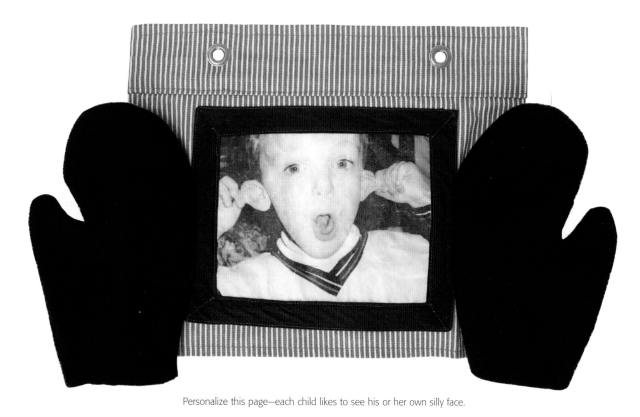

Personalize this page—each child likes to see his or her own silly face.

Peek-a-Boo Naptime

Tell when it's time for naptime. Children can practice telling time and then wake up the familiar napper.

Instead of using the clock only to identify naptime, kids can use it to identify times for various activities, like eating, sleeping, playing, whatever! Kids can adjust the clock to a certain time and then adjust the turn wheel to the appropriate activity.

What You'll Need

- ½ yard of bottom-weight background fabric
- ¼ yard of fast2fuse or regular fusible interfacing
  (If using fast2fuse, you also need a 2½″ × 14″ strip of regular fusible interfacing.)
- ¼ yard of fleece
- PhotoFabric sheet or iron-on transfer sheet and cotton fabric suitable to receive the iron-on
- Digital photo
- Thread
- 1 small (¼″ to ⅜″) button

How-To

Cutting

- Cut a 15″ × 23½″ rectangle of background fabric.
- Cut fast2fuse or interfacing per the instructions on pages 7–8.
- Cut 2 rectangles 3″ × 2″ of cotton fabric (use the background fabric or another scrap) for clock hands.
- Cut a 3″ × 2″ rectangle of fast2fuse for clock hands.
- Cut a 6″ × 7″ rectangle of fleece.

Assembly

1. **Iron on interfacing.** Follow the instructions for fast2fuse or fusible interfacing on page 7.

2. **Print photo.** Resize the photo to print no larger than 5″ wide by 6″ high. Leaving at least ½″ margins around the photo, follow the manufacturer's instructions to print the photo on PhotoFabric or transfer it to fabric and make it colorfast.

3. **Attach photo to page face.** Press under ¼″ around all 4 edges. Position the photo on the right half of the page face approximately 1″ in from the top and right edges. Pin in place. Edgestitch to secure the photo on all 4 sides.

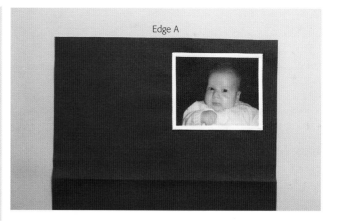

Edge A

4. **Attach fleece blanket**. Pin the fleece rectangle to completely cover the photo. Edgestitch around the lower part of each side and across the bottom edge.

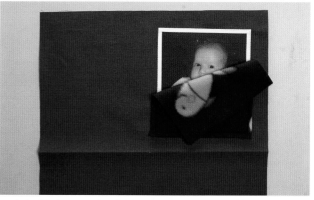

Stitch the blanket enough to hold it in place but make sure it can still be flipped back to reveal the photo of the child.

5. **Draw or print clock face**. If you prefer to make a clock by hand, use a paint pen to draw a clock face 5″ in diameter onto the background fabric (or other fabric to attach to the page face).

   If you prefer to use a computer, design a clock face 5″ in diameter and print it to PhotoFabric. Follow the manufacturer's instructions to print the image and make it colorfast. Leaving ½″ around the edges to press under, trim excess from around the clock face.

TIP Even if you make a round clock face, print it on a square background so it's easier to press the edges under.

6. Attach clock face to page face. Press under ¼″ around all the edges of the clock. Position the clock in the center of the other half of the page face. Pin and edgestitch the clock to the page face.

Cut 2 slits in an **X** or punch 2 small holes in the wide end of each clock hand. Sew a button in the center of the clock face and, using the slits like buttonholes, attach the clock hands to the clock.

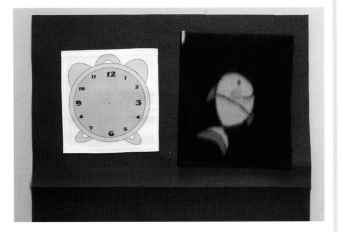

7. Attach clock hands. Fuse the 3″ x 2″ cotton rectangles to both sides of the fast2fuse rectangle. Following the patterns, cut 2 clock hands out of the stiffened cotton. Spiff up your clock hands by zigzagging around the edges.

8. Finish page. Follow the Completing the Page instructions (page 61) to complete the page.

Zigzagging the edges keeps them neat.

 If you have trouble zigzagging around the edges of the clock hands after you cut them out, zigzag *before* you cut them out and then trim off the excess. This method isn't as tidy, but it's easier.

Small clock hand pattern

Large clock hand pattern

Felt Board

The fold-out pocket extension on this felt board holds as many felt pieces as you care to cut out. Even randomly snipped felt shapes are enough to spark a child's imagination.

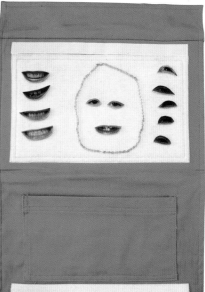

Cheap necklace chains stitched to the felt are a great way to "draw" a face. For facial features, you can print real features from photographs onto PhotoFabric and then glue the PhotoFabric features to felt. My kids love to mix one kid's eye with a different kid's eye and another kid's mouth.

What You'll Need

- ■ ¾ yard of bottom-weight background fabric
- ■ ¼ yard of heavyweight fast2fuse
- ■ 2½" × 15" strip of regular fusible interfacing
- ■ ¼ yard of felt (Felt on the bolt is more durable than individual felt sheets.)
- ■ 12" strip of ¾"-sew-on hook-and-loop tape
- ■ Different color felt sheets for shapes
- ■ Thread

How-To

Cutting

- ■ Cut a 40½" × 15" rectangle of background fabric.
- ■ Cut a 7½" × 11" rectangle of the background fabric for a pocket.
- ■ Cut the fast2fuse per the instructions on page 7.
- ■ Cut a 7" × 12" rectangle of felt.

Assembly

1. **Iron on fast2fuse**. Follow the instructions for fast2fuse on page 7. I recommend the heavyweight fast2fuse because it makes such a nice stiff board. Even though the background fabric is cut longer than a regular page, you can follow the same instructions. Affix the fast2fuse and regular fusible interfacing at the ends and disregard the extra length of fabric in between.

2. **Attach bristly side of hook-and-loop tape strip**. Pin the 12" strip of the bristly side of the hook-and-loop tape ¾" below and parallel to the top edge of the page face. Sew the bristly strip into place.

TIP To avoid snagging when the page is open, put the bristly side on the page top so the soft side will be rubbing against children's clothes.

3. **Attach felt background**. Position the 7" × 12" rectangle of felt on the page face so that the top edge of the felt is adjacent to the edge of the bristly hook-and-loop tape near the top edge of the page face. Pin the felt in place.

4. **Sew felt background on**. Given the thickness of the fast2fuse, you should reduce the pressure on the presser foot before stitching the felt to minimize stretching as you stitch. Edgestitch and double stitch around all 4 edges of the felt. Reset the presser foot pressure to normal before proceeding.

Edge A

5. **Make pocket for felt pieces**. Using the 7½" × 11" rectangle of the background fabric, follow the instructions on page 8 to make the pocket, using an 11" edge at the top of the pocket.

6. **Position pocket**. Position the pocket 2" below the bottom of the felt and centered side-to-side, with the pocket opening toward the felt piece. Pin the pocket in place. Edgestitch and double stitch around the side and bottom edges.

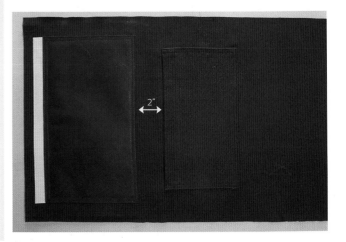
2"

7. Finish the page *almost* like the other pages. With wrong sides together, press down the ¹/₂″ margin above the thin strip of fusible interfacing. Align Edges A and B following the Completing the Page instructions (page 61), and pin the side seams. Make sure Edge A is behind Edge B and both raw edges are together. Your side seams will be much longer for this page because of the extension. Using ¹/₂″ seam allowances, stitch the side seams. Clip the corners and turn the page right side out. Poke out the corners and press the edges. Be careful to keep the iron away from the felt, which could melt at high temperatures.

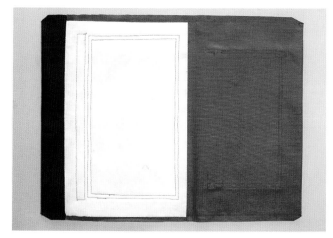

8. Add finishing touches. Edgestitch and double stitch the page closed along the top of the page face. Press the backside of the page, fusing the fast2fuse to the back of the page face. Position the other 12″ strip of hook-and-loop tape on the front, along the bottom edge of the extended page, below the pocket, and centered side-to-side. Pin in place and stitch.

9. Edgestitch and double stitch sides and top edge of page. You do not need to edgestitch the bottom, because the stitching on the hook-and-loop tape already secures the bottom edge.

10. Mark and stitch buttonholes.

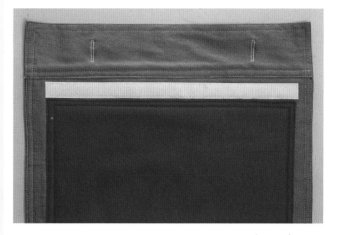

11. Add felt pieces to pocket. Make various sets of felt pieces and put them in separate plastic bags to be rotated into the pocket. Make sets for various holidays or favorite themes, like flowers, bugs, aliens, faces, construction, dress up, castles, or whatever your kids might like.

Hook-and-loop tape holds the pocket closed so the felt pieces stay in place.

Ask your children to help cut out the shapes. My kids love cutting out the faces and the abstract shapes, and they do a great job. And don't worry about making the felt pieces perfect. Kids will put them together in combinations you couldn't imagine anyway!

Magnet Board

This page is a favorite for kids of all ages. More than once, I've watched kids cry trying to get the magnets away from an interested dad. Plus, if you ever end up sitting in metal folding chairs, your magnetic options are endless.

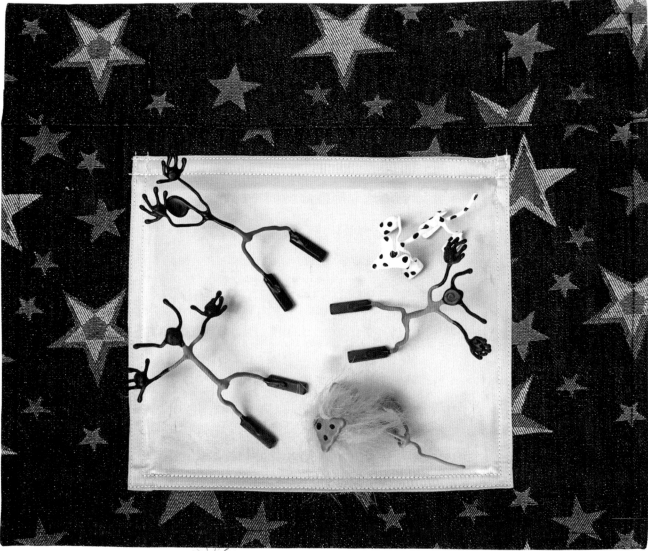

What You'll Need

- ½ yard of bottom-weight background fabric
- ¼ yard of fast2fuse
- 2½" × 15" strip of regular fusible interfacing
- ¼ yard of lightweight fabric (*I used a silver-colored satin lining fabric to make it look metallic.*)

- 5¾" × 7" metal nail-on mending plate (also called a tie plate)
- Electrical tape
- Thread
- Magnetic toys

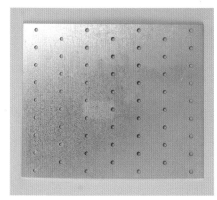

Mending plates are available at hardware and building supply stores.

How-To

Cutting

- Cut a 15″ × 23 $\frac{1}{2}$ ″ rectangle of background fabric.
- Cut an 8″ × 8″ square of background fabric for pocket.
- Cut the fast2fuse per the instructions on page 7.
- Cut an 8″ × 9 $\frac{1}{4}$ ″ rectangle of lightweight fabric.

Assembly

1. **Iron on fast2fuse.** Follow the instructions for fast2fuse on page 7.

2. **Make back pocket.** Using the 8″ × 8″ square of the background fabric, follow the instructions on page 8 to make the pocket.

3. **Attach pocket to back of page.** Position the pocket on the back of the page. Center the pocket 4″ from each side and 1 $\frac{1}{2}$ ″ from the fold. Make sure that the top of the pocket is facing away from the fold. Pin in place and then edgestitch and double stitch the side and bottom edges of the pocket.

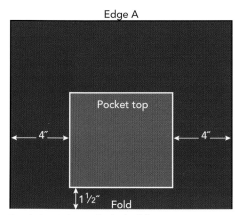

Attach the pocket to the back of the page.

4. **Wrap metal plate edges.** Cover an edge on the front of the metal plate with half of the electrical tape strip. Wrap the other half of the tape strip to the back of the metal plate. Repeat for all 4 edges.

Double wrap each corner diagonally with tape.

5. **Make lightweight fabric pocket to cover metal plate.** Press under $\frac{1}{2}$ ″ around all 4 sides of the silver fabric rectangle. Position the rectangle in the center of the page face. Pin in place and edgestitch 3 sides.

TIP

To mark a fold line, baste with $\frac{1}{2}$ ″ seam allowances around the 4 edges of the silver fabric. After pressing, remove the basting.

Place the metal plate over the pocket to make sure you have enough space to insert the plate. Double stitch the same 3 sides of the silver fabric rectangle.

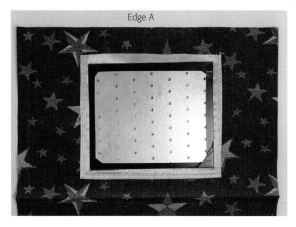
Edge A

If your pocket is too small, double stitch closer to the first row of stitching.

6. Insert metal plate and stitch pocket closed. Insert the metal plate into the silver pocket. Pin the pocket closed along the fourth edge.

Attach the zipper foot to your sewing machine. To make sewing easier, hold the plate flat so it doesn't pull away from the presser foot as you sew and the weight shifts. Edgestitch and double stitch the fourth side.

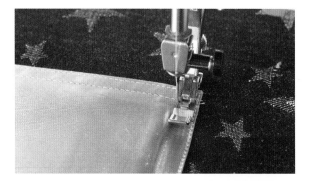

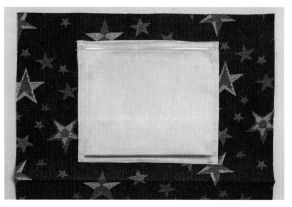

7. Finish page. Follow the Completing the Page instructions (page 61) to finish the page.

8. Put magnetic toys in back pocket. Add a couple magnets or magnetic toys to the pocket on the back.

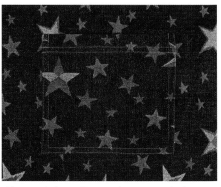
The metal plate will attract the magnets in the pocket so they will stay in place.

Multiple small magnets inside the pocket can substitute for the metal plate.

Bear in mind that magnets could cause an adverse effect with computerized sewing machines.

1. Attach the 3 sides of the pockets following the directions and then stitch 2 vertical dividing lines.

2. Insert 3 small magnets and then stitch a horizontal dividing line to keep those magnets in place.

3. Insert 3 more magnets and then stitch another horizontal line.

4. Insert 3 more magnets and then double stitch the top of the pocket closed.

Happy Family Game

We invented this game for when bickering at our house got a bit out of hand. It's a reminder of how each person's actions impact everyone in the house, and the personalized cards always help us laugh instead of cry about our foibles.

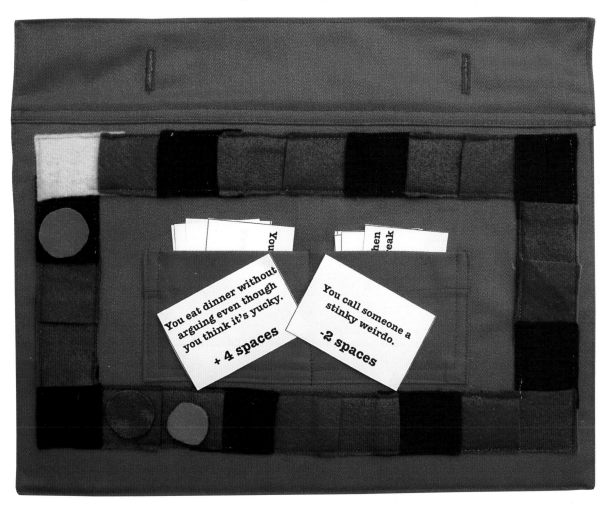

What You'll Need

- ½ yard of bottom-weight background fabric
- ¼ yard of heavyweight fast2fuse
- 2½" × 15" strip of regular fusible interfacing
- Several different colored felt pieces
- Cardstock to print personalized game cards
- Thread

How-To

Cutting

- Cut a 15" × 23½" rectangle of background fabric.
- Cut a 5" × 9" rectangle of background fabric for the pocket.
- Cut fast2fuse per the instructions on page 7.
- Cut 24 felt rectangles 1½" × 1" for the game board.
- Cut a few small pieces of felt for game tokens.

Assembly

1. **Iron on fast2fuse**. Follow the instructions for fast2fuse on page 8.

2. **Make pocket**. Follow the instructions on page 8 to make the 5″ × 9″ rectangle into a pocket, using a 9″ edge at the top of the pocket.

3. **Attach pocket**. Position the pocket in the center and 2½″ from the bottom edge of the page face. Pin in place. Edgestitch and double stitch the side and bottom edges of the pocket. Stitch a dividing line through the middle of the pocket.

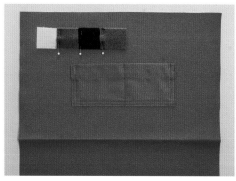

Leave enough room around the pockets to make the game board.

4. **Attach felt pieces**. Position the felt rectangles around the 2 pockets to make a rectangular path. Overlap one end of each rectangle over the previous rectangle. Pin in place and edgestitch.

Adjust rectangles as necessary to complete the path.

 TIP Though it seems silly and obvious, talking about our habits and their impact on our whole family helps us to be more aware of how each person contributes to the overall happiness of our home.

5. **Finish page**. Follow the Completing the Page instructions (page 61) to finish the page.

6. **Make personalized game cards**. On cardstock, print 2″ × 3″ game cards with personalized good and bad habits. Give each habit a plus or minus value to indicate how many squares you go forward or backward. Good habits move the player forward. Bad habits move the player backward.

 TIP Print a long list of cards at one time. It's fun to rotate them in and out to keep the game different.

Here are some of the cards we use and their values:

- **You burp at the table: –1 space**
- **You bug someone for fun: –2 spaces**
- **You leave your dirty clothes on the bathroom floor: –1 space**
- **You make your bed: +2 spaces**
- **You put all your toys away: +2 spaces**
- **You brush your teeth without being told: +4 spaces**
- **You clean up after your snack: +2 spaces**

 TIP The most personalized cards are the favorites at my house. My boys love when Mom draws the "You burp at the table" card.

7. **Put cards and tokens in the pockets, and play!** To prevent bickering, a single token can represent the whole family, so if 2 or more people are playing together, they move the single token forward or backward as indicated on the cards. When one person wins, the whole family wins!

 TIP If you prefer a game that doesn't require reading, make different colored cards to correspond with the colors of the game board. A child can then play alone by drawing a card and moving the token to that color. This version is better for places where kids have to be silent and can't have help reading.

Completing the Page

After you have completed a page using the instructions specific to an activity, follow these instructions to complete the page.

1. Press Edge B down. Press under ½″ of fabric along Edge B so that wrong sides are together.

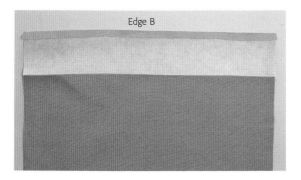

2. Fold page closed. Place the fabric right side up with Edge A at the bottom. Fold up Edge A 9″ along the edge of the page face and the big piece of fast2fuse or fusible interfacing. Right sides will be together, and the activity will be hidden inside.

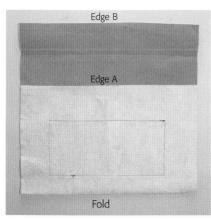

The big rectangle of interfacing marks the fold line at the edge of the page face.

Fold Edge B down 2½″ so that right sides are together inside the fold.

Tuck the folded Edge B **behind** Edge A so that raw Edges A and B are together.

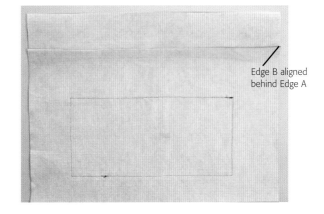

Edge B aligned behind Edge A

3. Stitch side seams. Making sure Edge A is aligned behind Edge B, pin the page sides together. Stitch the sides using ½″ seam allowances.

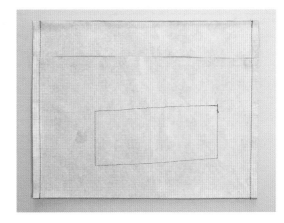

4. Turn page right side out. Clip the corners and turn the page right side out. Press all 4 edges of the page.

5. Edgestitch page closed. Edgestitch Edge B over Edge A to close the page along Edge B.

6. Topstitch edges. Topstitch around the 4 sides of the page.

TIP

You can choose to edgestitch, topstitch, or double stitch. I like the look of the double stitching the best, but you can decide based on your preference and how close to the edge of the page face the activity extends.

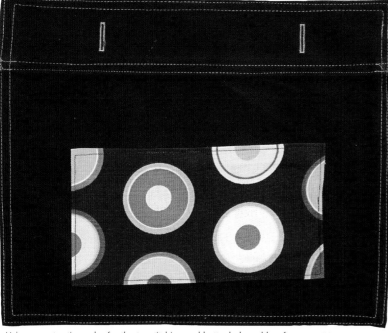

Using a contrasting color for the topstitching and buttonholes adds a fun accent to any page.

7. Mark and sew buttonholes. For each buttonhole, make a mark approximately $3\frac{1}{2}''$ from each side edge and $\frac{3}{4}''$ from the top edge. Sew 1″ buttonholes. Slit the buttonholes open. *Option:* You can use grommets instead of making buttonholes.

We always take our pages apart to share, so binder rings or carabiners are a perfect way to hold pages together just long enough to get the book to wherever we're going.

8. Attach pages. Loop binder rings (sold at office supply stores) or carabiners through the buttonholes to attach the pages together.

About the Author

Michelle Van Tassell loves to create with fabric, lumber, and words. She regularly sews clothing, costumes, and quiet books; she occasionally builds furniture, climbing walls, and playhouses; and she loves to write. Michelle has a master's degree in American Studies and is working on a Ph.D. in English literature.

Sources

Crafter's Images PhotoFabric
Blumenthal Craft
1929 Main St.
Lansing, IA 52151
(563) 538-4211
www.blumenthallansing.com

fast2fuse Double-Sided Interfacing
C&T Publishing
P.O. Box 1456
Lafayette, CA 94549
(800) 284-1114
www.ctpub.com

Funky Fur
Grafix
19499 Miles Rd.
Cleveland, OH 44128
(800) 447-2349
www.grafixarts.com

Just Another Button Company
116 W. Market St.
Troy, IL 62294
(618) 667-8531
www.justanotherbuttoncompany.com

Quilter's Vinyl
C&T Publishing
P.O. Box 1456
Lafayette, CA 94549
(800) 284-1114
www.ctpub.com

WonderUnder
Pellon Consumer Products
4720A Stone Dr.
Tucker, GA 30084
(770) 491-8001
www.shoppellon.com

For a list of other fine books from C&T Publishing, ask for a free catalog:
C&T Publishing
P.O. Box 1456
Lafayette, CA 94549
(800) 284-1114
www.ctpub.com

C&T Publishing's professional photography services are now available to the public. Visit us at www.ctmediaservices.com

For quilting supplies:
Cotton Patch
1025 Brown Ave.
Lafayette, CA 94549
(800) 835-4418
www.quiltusa.com

NOTE

Because fabric manufacturers keep most fabrics in print for only a short time, fabrics and notions used in the projects shown may not be currently available.

Great Titles
from C&T PUBLISHING

photo FUN
Print Your Own Fabric for Quilts & Crafts

The Hewlett-Packard Company · Edited by Cyndy Lyle Rymer

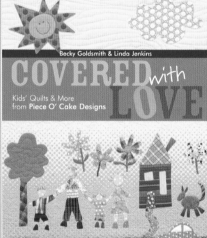

Becky Goldsmith & Linda Jenkins

COVERED with LOVE

Kids' Quilts & More from Piece O' Cake Designs

QUILTER'S Vinyl

Ideal for Appliqué Overlays, Quilting Designs & Crafts

fast fun & easy FABRIC CRITTER BAGS

Mary Link

From Stuff Stashers to Beach Bags to Pillowcases

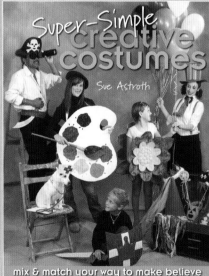

Super-Simple creative costumes

Sue Astroth

mix & match your way to make believe

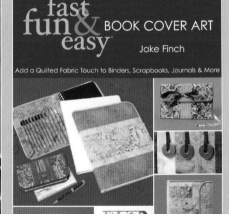

fast fun & easy BOOK COVER ART

Jake Finch

Add a Quilted Fabric Touch to Binders, Scrapbooks, Journals & More